CHRISTMAS

CONTENTS

Frosty The Snowman	2
Have Yourself A Merry Little Christmas	4
I Saw Mommy Kissing Santa Claus	6
Little Donkey	8
The Little Drummer Boy	16
Mary's Boy Child	10
Mistletoe And Wine	12
Sleigh Ride	14

Arranged by BARRIE CARSON TURNER

First published 1991
©International Music Publications
Southend Road, Woodford Green,
Essex IG8 8HN, England.

215-2-633

FROSTY THE SNOWMAN

Words and Music by
STEVE NELSON and JACK ROLLINS

4

HAVE YOURSELF A MERRY LITTLE CHRISTMAS

Words and Music by
HUGH MARTIN and RALPH BLANE

© 1944 & 1991 EMI Feist Catalogue Inc., USA
EMI United Partnership Ltd., London WC2H 0EA

I SAW MOMMY KISSING SANTA CLAUS

Words and Music by
TOMMIE CONNOR

LITTLE DONKEY

Words and Music by
ERIC BOSWELL

MARY'S BOY CHILD

Words and Music by
JESTER HAIRSTON

MISTLETOE AND WINE

Words by LESLIE STEWART and JEREMY PAUL
Music by KEITH STRACHAN

17 𝄌 **With more movement**

SLEIGH RIDE

Words by MITCHELL PARISH
Music by LEROY ANDERSON

THE LITTLE DRUMMER BOY

Words and Music by
HARRY SIMEONE, HENRY ONORATI
and KATHERINE K DAVIES